FULL-DAY KINDERGARTEN:
Exploring the Research

By James Elicker

© 2000 by Phi Delta Kappa International, Bloomington, Indiana 47402
All rights reserved. Published 2000
Printed in the United States of America
ISBN 0-87367-741-2

CONTENTS

Introduction 1
    Changing Families, Changing Schools 1
    Importance of the Early Years 1
    Appropriate Practice in Kindergarten 2
    Definitions 3

Full-Day Kindergarten: Claims and Counterclaims 3

Reviews of Full-Day Kindergarten Research, 1970-1997 4
    Full Day Meta-Analysis 5
    Long-Term Effects 5
    Research Limitations 5

Recent Full-Day Kindergarten Research 6
    What Do They Do All Day? 6
    Comparison of Full-Day, Alternate-Day, and Half-Day Kindergarten ... 7

Conclusions 8
    Implications for Administrators, Teachers, and Parents 9
    Promoting Consideration of Full-Day Kindergarten 10

Endnotes 11

Resources 13
    Books and Articles 13
    Websites 14

INTRODUCTION

Throughout the United States, the availability of full-day kindergarten is expanding, both in public schools and private schools. From 1970 to 1997, the percentage of all five-year-olds enrolled in any public or private preprimary school program grew 20%, from 69% in 1970 to 89% in 1997.[1] The percentage of five-year-olds enrolled in *full-day* programs rose from 12% in 1970 to 42% in 1990 to 55% in 1997. Despite this dramatic increase, initial discussions about whether to offer public full-day kindergarten provoke controversy in many communities. In these debates, parents, teachers, administrators, and others may tout the many benefits of full-day kindergarten or question the expense of hiring additional teachers and providing more classroom space.

It is clear that the number of children enrolled in full-day kindergarten has increased steadily over the past three decades. What are the reasons for this increase, and why does the issue of full-day kindergarten continue to provoke controversy? Reasons for schools to consider expanding their early childhood programs, including full-day kindergarten, include

- the increasing needs of families for expanded early childhood education and child-care services;
- an increasing awareness among parents and educators of the importance of the early years for brain development; and
- debates among educators about what constitutes developmentally appropriate instruction in kindergarten.

Changing Families, Changing Schools

Most parents of five-year-old children in the United States now work full time outside the home.[2] Parents desire high-quality educational programs for their kindergarten-age children. They do not want their five-year-olds in two or three different care and education settings each day, and they do not want to transport them among those settings. Further, many children have already spent several years in full-day child care and education programs before they enter kindergarten, so they are well adapted to a school-like setting for a full day. Parents recognize the potential of elementary schools to provide kindergarten for the full school day. Across the country, many parents are now urging schools to provide kindergarten for six hours or more per day.

Importance of the Early Years

Recent research in brain development is reinforcing what early educators have suspected for years — the first few years of life are a sensitive period for many types of learning and behavioral development.[3] From prenatal development through the early childhood years, appropriate sensory and cognitive stimulation, challenging learning experiences, and emotional support are essential for optimal development of children's neural networks and information processing abilities.

Coupled with this renewed interest in children's early learning potentials is the rising concern of many teachers about children's readiness to enter elementary school. In a recent national survey of 3,600 kindergarten teachers, Robert Pianta and his associates at the National Center for Early Development and Learning (NCEDL) found that nearly one-half of these teachers had serious concerns about the children entering their classrooms each fall.[4]

Visit the website of the National Association for the Education of Young Children at **www.naeyc.org** to learn more about issues surrounding education for young learners.

The most frequently cited problem was children's inability to follow directions (46%), followed by low pre-academic skills (36%), inability to work independently (34%), inability to work in a group (30%), and inability to communicate effectively (14%). Teachers also cited issues involving the home environment (35%), lack of formal preschool experiences (31%), and children's immaturity (20%).

Concerns about school transition were expressed most frequently by kindergarten teachers in urban schools with high poverty levels and in schools with high proportions of minority students. Less experienced teachers also perceived higher rates of school entry problems than did more experienced teachers. The results of this large-scale study suggest that children enter kindergarten with a wide range of skills and problems and that more experienced and skilled teachers may perceive some of these differences as normal and expected. The NCEDL researchers concluded that, while many children are not completely ready to learn when they enter kindergarten, there may be cultural or ethnic mismatches between some teachers and their kindergarten students, especially in urban, low-income, minority schools. Such mismatches can result in increased reports of problems associated with following directions, communicating, social skills, and immaturity.

Fueled by new evidence that lost learning opportunities in the early years may be difficult to regain and by teachers' perceptions that many children enter kindergarten not optimally ready to learn, decision makers are increasingly focusing attention on the quality and effectiveness of their kindergarten programs. This scrutiny often leads to the question, Are two or three hours per day in the kindergarten year really enough to bring about optimal learning and early school adjustment?

Appropriate Practice in Kindergarten

Early childhood and primary-level educators have debated for years the most appropriate methods for teaching kindergarten.[5] As policymakers consider whether to move to full-day kindergarten, many questions concerning program goals, class size, and curriculum naturally arise, such as

- What is the purpose of kindergarten?
- How can a teacher effectively assess and meet each child's educational needs, when she or he is with 40 to 60 children each day (combined morning and afternoon classes) for only two and one-half hours?
- How can kindergarten teachers accomplish everything that is expected of them before children enter first grade?
- How will the additional three to four hours each day in a full-day class be used?
- Will basic skills instruction in literacy and mathematics now used in first and second grade be inappropriately pushed down to kindergarten?
- Is acceleration of academic achievement the goal of full-day kindergarten, or is it to deepen and enrich the educational experiences of children?

These questions are not exclusive to scheduling, but proponents and opponents of full-day kindergarten often raise them. This summary explores the issue of kindergarten scheduling by examining claims about the benefits and detriments of full-day kindergarten, findings from research, and reasonable approaches for teachers and administrators.

A network of educational resources and materials from the Kindergarten Connection website can be found at www.kconnect.com

Definitions

I use the term *full-day kindergarten* to describe kindergarten classes offered five days a week for five to six hours each day. This type of program is also called *all-day kindergarten* or *extended-day kindergarten* in the professional literature and in schools. *Half-day kindergarten* describes programs that meet five days a week for two and one-half to three hours each day. *Alternate-day kindergarten* describes programs that meet every other day — two or three times a week — for five to six hours each day.

FULL-DAY KINDERGARTEN: CLAIMS AND COUNTERCLAIMS

Proponents of full-day kindergarten claim that attending school for an entire school day offers children additional benefits beyond the half-day program.[6] It is assumed that children will gain more benefits with additional time to participate in stimulating educational experiences. Some maintain that increasing the amount and quality of the kindergarten experience will result in higher overall academic achievement and lower rates of placement in special education programs, especially for children who enter school with fewer preschool advantages.[7] However, other advocates assert that the true value of a full day is not in its potential to accelerate learning or to cover more academic content, but in the opportunity to allow children to experience the kindergarten curriculum more richly at a less hurried pace.[8]

Supporters argue that with fewer children to teach and care for each day, full-day kindergarten teachers are better able to assess educational needs and to individualize instruction, providing a richer, more appropriate education for each child.[9] Furthermore, when kindergarten children are in the school building all day, they have more opportunities to participate in the broader school program, including special events and enrichment activities.[10] In general, proponents claim that a full day allows for a more expansive curriculum for kindergarten students.

According to advocates, the families of full-day kindergarten students enjoy advantages, too. Reductions in child-care costs, settings, and daily transitions may be beneficial for both children and parents. Children in full-day kindergarten can travel on the same schedule to the same settings as their older siblings rather than having an entirely separate routine, reducing the complications for children and families. A final potential advantage for parents is that full-day kindergarten teachers, working with 20 to 25 students each day instead of 40 to 50, are better able to establish and maintain collaborative relationships with parents.

Depending on local circumstances, schools may find that full-day kindergarten classrooms are advantageous in other ways. If space for additional classrooms is available, staff and parents are strongly supportive, and state funding is provided, the decision to finance and implement a full-day program can be relatively easy. Some administrators find that scheduling school events is simplified and costs for transportation are reduced when busses are not needed to transport kindergarten children in the middle of the day. Another potential financial advantage for public schools in some locales is that families may transfer their kindergarten-age children from private schools to public schools when full-day kindergarten is offered, thereby increasing enrollment.

While advocates identify many advantages to full-day kindergarten, opponents identify a number of disadvantages.[11] For example, some suggest that adjustment to school may be more difficult for young children attending classes all day. Less mature children may become tired, frustrated, or stressed with a full day of school. Intense, formal academic instruction

---

The full text of the research report "Full-Day or Half-Day Kindergarten?" is available at **www.ed.gov/databases/ERIC_Digests/ed256474.html**

may be introduced too early or inappropriately. Parents who want to spend more time with their children at home may feel unnecessarily pressured to send them to school for a full day. Additional teaching staff members are required for full-day kindergarten, perhaps without additional funding for the school's operating budget. More classroom space, more equipment, and more supplies are required. Are these disadvantages likely? And if so, are the costs of full-day kindergarten worth the benefits?

REVIEWS OF FULL-DAY KINDERGARTEN RESEARCH, 1970-1997

Over the past 30 years, school evaluators and university researchers have attempted to determine the impact of full-day kindergarten compared with other scheduling arrangements, especially the traditional half day. Most of this research has focused on academic achievement as measured by standardized test scores. Achievement outcomes are typically assessed at the end of the kindergarten year, sometimes during first grade. Until recently, the evidence for clear benefits of the full-day schedule has been inconclusive, according to reviews of this research.

A number of early research reviews concluded that students enrolled in full-day kindergarten exhibit at least short-term academic gains compared to students participating in the half-day or alternate-day schedules. A 1982 review of eight studies on the effects of three kindergarten schedules on academic achievement revealed that 85% of the studies found short-term academic gains for students enrolled in a full-day schedule, and 15% found no differences between the three schedules.[12] Vincent Puleo concluded that full-day programs produced greater academic gains than half-day programs.[13] While there was not overwhelming evidence for significant, long-lasting quantitative benefits, many studies identified other advantages to full-day kindergarten, including increases in academic skills and instructional time and qualitative advantages reported by teachers and parents.

While there is inconsistent evidence that *all* students enrolled in full-day kindergarten experience academic gains, there is stronger support that disadvantaged students or students at risk for school failure benefit from the full-day schedule. Nancy Karweit concluded that underachieving and disadvantaged students consistently experienced short-term benefits from full-day kindergarten.[14] A review by Patrick Bickers of studies comparing the effects of full- and half-day programs on academic achievement found significant benefits for disadvantaged students attending full-day kindergarten.[15] (In all of these studies, most teachers reported they favored full-day kindergarten.) No reviews of research have identified consistent academic advantages for the traditional half-day schedule compared to the full-day schedule.

Alternate-day schedules are sometimes implemented in rural school districts to reduce transportation costs or scheduling complications. A number of studies have shown that there are academic or behavior advantages for children attending alternate-day schedules compared to the traditional half-day program. However, there has been little evidence that alternate-day programs are superior to full-day programs in terms of student academic or social growth.[16] Only two studies, one by Charlene Hildebrand and another by Dominic Gullo, have compared all three scheduling options (half-day, full-day, alternate-day) using the same design.[17] The more recent of these is reviewed in some detail later.

Visit the website of the International Reading Association at **www.reading.org/publications/books/lssv1_2.htm** to find out how to order *Literacy Instruction in Half- and Whole-Day Kindergarten: Research to Practice.*

Full Day Meta-Analysis

In the most recent comprehensive review of research, Joseph Fusaro examined 23 studies published between 1974 and 1991 that assessed the academic achievement of full-day kindergarten students compared to half-day students.[18] Fusaro was the first to employ quantitative meta-analytic techniques to determine whether there are significant overall effects favoring full-day programs. Meta-analysis is a statistical analysis that involves averaging the effect size of multiple studies of the same research question to establish an overall effect size. On the basis of Fusaro's meta-analysis, he concluded that children who attend full-day programs show significantly greater achievement than those who attend half-day programs. He further concluded that the effect size for full-day programs was substantial, with participation in full-day kindergarten accounting for 59% to 62% of the difference in academic achievement between the two groups.

Long-Term Effects

Few well-designed studies have examined the effects of full-day kindergarten beyond the first grade. For example, of the 23 studies included in Fusaro's meta-analysis, only two assessed student achievement beyond first grade, with conflicting results.

Research Limitations

While the results of Fusaro's meta-analysis may seem quite conclusive, he correctly cautions that few full-day kindergarten studies have employed true experimental designs. This means that researchers have not randomly selected full- and half-day classes or randomly assigned students to full-day and half-day classes, nor have they carefully controlled the program "treatment"— teacher qualifications, curriculum, or learning activities. Further, few studies have used pretests to establish students' abilities at the beginning of the school year. Therefore, it is possible that there were pre-existing differences in children's academic abilities that accounted for the subsequent differences found between full- and half-day schedules. (Parents with higher socioeconomic status may be more likely to enroll their children in full-day kindergarten earlier and, thus, their children may be disproportionately represented.)

It is also possible that factors other than the length of the school day, such as teachers' skills or philosophies or certain curricula produced some of the observed gains. These factors are seldom documented or controlled.[19] Nancy Karweit also speculates that when programs shift from half- to full-day, the kindergarten curriculum may often become more academic. Such a curriculum change alone could account for achievement gains made by full-day students. A final problem is the over-reliance on group-administered academic achievement tests to assess outcomes for children on a full-day schedule. Problems with the validity of such structured tests for young children are well documented.[20] Some advocates claim that the benefits of full-day kindergarten go far beyond gains in achievement test scores. Personal and social adjustment and other aspects of healthy adaptation to school have seldom been assessed in full-day kindergarten research to date.

While there is a clear pattern of higher achievement and other benefits for students in full-day kindergarten, there is still some uncertainty that the length of the school day alone is the factor that resulted in the documented gains. For example, of the 20 studies Karweit reviewed, 17 used pre-existing "convenience" samples, that is, families who volunteered to participate.[21] Of the 23 studies in Fusaro's meta-analysis, more than half neither randomly

---

Find out about the full-day kindergarten program at the Evansville-Vanderburgh Schools by visiting their website at **www.evsc.k12.in.us/evscinfo/kindergarten/contents.html**

assigned students nor statistically controlled for pre-existing differences in academic skills. In many studies, the researchers simply assessed the progress of children who happened to be enrolled in half- and full-day classes. Another conclusion to be drawn from previous research is that many of the potential benefits of full-day programs simply have not been carefully examined.

RECENT FULL-DAY KINDERGARTEN RESEARCH

Two recent studies have attempted to overcome the limitations of previous research by employing true experimental or quasi-experimental designs and by controlling for children's pre-existing abilities and variations in teachers' skills or philosophies. These researchers also observed a wide range of student activities and outcomes, including academic achievement and other aspects of school adjustment.

What Do They Do All Day?

In our research at Purdue University, we conducted a two-year evaluation of a newly implemented full-day program in a stable middle-class suburban community in Wisconsin, comparing it to the existing half-day program.[22] This study employed a true experimental design, so children were randomly selected and assigned to the new full-day kindergarten option. Teachers in the study were carefully matched for professional training, experience, and teaching philosophy. Pre-existing differences in the children and their families were statistically controlled in the analyses.

In this study, we focused on what actually occurs in full- and half-day classrooms. We documented the quality of engagement and the amount of time children spent in learning activities throughout the day, assessed academic outcomes at the end of the kindergarten year, and repeatedly interviewed parents and teachers to gain insights into their perspectives. This school district described both its full- and half-day kindergarten curricula as "developmentally appropriate," a claim mostly supported by our observations.

We found that children in full-day classrooms spent considerably more time in both absolute and relative terms engaged in self-initiated learning activities (e.g., play or learning centers). (See Figure 1.) They also spent more time in direct one-to-one teaching situations, including small-group instruction — the teacher working with two to eight children — and individual teacher-structured work, for example, writing in journals or completing other teacher-assigned tasks. Children in half-day classrooms, on the other hand, spent the majority of their time in teacher-led, whole-class instructional activities. The more balanced array of learning activities experienced by full-day students — a mix of teacher-directed and child-initiated learning — is more consistent with the recommendations for developmentally appropriate practice of early childhood professional organizations, including the National Association for the Education of Young Children.[23]

Full-day students in our study also demonstrated significantly higher report card achievement in literacy, math, general learning, and social skills at the end of the kindergarten year. Finally, full-day students were rated by their teachers as being more advanced in readiness for first grade.

Parents and teachers perceived similar benefits when interviewed. Children in full-day classes were better able to initiate and engage flexibly in learning activities that were appropriate to their interests and skills according to teachers' reports. Teachers also found that they had more time to assess and plan for individual children's needs and to plan the integrative

Figure 1. Minutes per Day Spent on Activities in Full- and Half-Day Kindergarten Classrooms

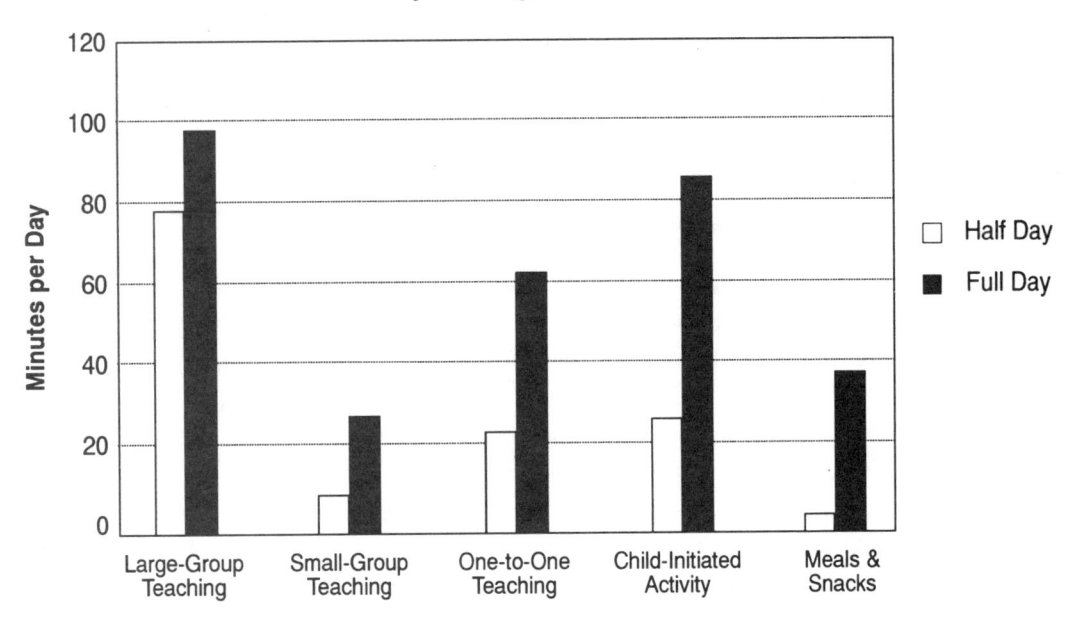

curriculum and more opportunities for one-to-one interactions with children and parents. Teachers in the full-day program said they could better meet the needs of children with a range of abilities, from those with disabilities to children who were developmentally advanced. Parents regarded the full-day program as less hurried, with opportunities for teachers to get to know their children better. They also appreciated the extra time children had to engage in social and creative activities, in addition to the traditional academic subjects.

Even though parents and teachers perceived many advantages to the full-day program, there were also high levels of parent satisfaction with the half-day program, suggesting that the overall quality of the kindergarten program in this school district was high. While most parents reported they would choose the full-day program in the future, a small percentage (28%) said they still preferred the half-day program at the end of the second year. Those favoring the half day said it allowed their child a more gradual adjustment to a full school day or that learning experiences at school and at home should be more balanced during the kindergarten year. These parent perspectives suggest the desirability of maintaining a half-day kindergarten option in some communities for families who have their own educational resources and want to spend more time with their five-year-olds.

Finally, we examined the impact of the full-day kindergarten on families' use of child care. We found that the need for child care was not entirely eliminated, even though the number of hours of care needed beyond the kindergarten day (and thus cost) was reduced for families participating in full-day kindergarten. Most families still needed to arrange before- or after-school child care. Such child-care programs are increasingly available for elementary school students on site or near school buildings, making all-day arrangements more convenient.

Comparison of Full-Day, Alternate-Day, and Half-Day Kindergarten

Charlene Hildebrand recently conducted a study comparing the impact of full-day, alternate-day, and half-day kindergarten scheduling on children's academic and social competencies.[24] The kindergarten classrooms were in three schools in one district that used a common kindergarten curriculum. Using a quasi-experimental design, the researcher statistically controlled for pre-existing differences among the groups in ages and achievement test scores in reading, writing, and math. The outcomes assessed were end-of-year scores on individually administered tests of reading, writing, math, and teachers' ratings of positive or negative classroom behaviors. Teacher philosophies were compared using a measure of teachers' beliefs about literacy. Teachers' use of developmentally appropriate practices (DAP) was assessed by making observations in each classroom.

Hildebrand found that during the kindergarten year full-day students made significantly greater gains in reading compared to half-day students after controlling for beginning reading ability. Gains for students in alternate-day kindergarten fell between those for students in the full- and half-day classrooms. There were no statistically significant differences between the three groups in writing and math achievement, although mean scores favored the full-day group. Assessments of teaching philosophy and classroom practices indicated that none of the teachers in this particular study was strongly invested in DAP, but the alternate-day teachers were using more practices considered developmentally appropriate. Interestingly, teachers' ratings of positive and negative classroom behaviors consistently favored the half-day group over both full-day groups, suggesting that while an all-day program promotes gains in achievement, it may present some additional challenges for teachers in child guidance and classroom management.

Hildebrand concluded that full-day and alternate-day kindergarten are superior to half-day kindergarten for gains in reading achievement. She suggested that children in full-day classes "benefit from additional time to engage in various experiences with alphabetic text while in the process of constructing their own understandings of written language." Evaluations of classroom behaviors consistently favored half-day students, in contrast to the research of Gullo and his colleagues, who found that children in alternate-day kindergarten programs displayed more pro-social and fewer negative classroom behaviors than children in half-day programs.[25] Clearly, the impact of kindergarten scheduling on children's social adjustment needs additional research attention. However, in our Wisconsin study we found no evidence that full-day kindergarten resulted in more stress or behavior problems for children.

CONCLUSIONS

Surveying the existing research, we can draw the following conclusions about full-day kindergarten:

- Students participating in full-day kindergarten consistently progress further academically during the kindergarten year, as assessed by achievement tests, than students in either half-day or alternate-day programs.
- There is tentative evidence that full-day kindergarten has stronger, longer-lasting academic benefits for children from low-income families or others with fewer educational resources prior to kindergarten.
- There is not current, strong evidence that the academic achievement gains of full-day kindergarten persist beyond first grade for all students.
- There is no evidence for detrimental effects of full-day kindergarten. The full-day curriculum, if developmentally appropriate for five- and six-year-olds, does not seem to overly stress or pressure kindergarten children.

Learn about the effects of full-day kindergarten on at-risk students by visiting the Pennsylvania Partnerships for Children website at www.papartnerships.org/fdkweb.htm

- Kindergarten teachers and parents strongly value the increased flexibility and opportunities to communicate and individualize instruction for children offered by the full-day schedule.

More research is needed to examine the long-term impact of full-day kindergarten. Also, more study is needed of full-day kindergarten effects on students' personal and social school adjustment and other aspects of learning not well documented by standardized achievement tests.

Traditional half-day kindergarten should remain an option for families who have educational resources, value the time at home during the day with their five-year-olds, and desire a more gradual introduction to formal schooling.

Implications for Administrators, Teachers, and Parents

Kindergarten education is being taken more seriously today than ever before. Changes in the lifestyles of American families, recent scientific evidence for the importance of the early years for brain development, and continuing debates about the most effective ways of educating young children have all helped focus renewed attention on kindergarten. Educators in many communities in the United States are considering whether to offer kindergarten for a full school day.

Proposals to implement full-day kindergarten often come first from parents. They are seeking relief from the patchwork of child care and education programs of uneven quality now available to their kindergarten child-each day. But they are also recognizing increasingly that a child's experience in the first year of formal schooling has implications beyond the kindergarten year.

Along with parents, teachers who keep current with national trends in education may advocate for full-day programs. Faced with ever-increasing demands to cover more curriculum content, they may be looking for more time each day to work with their kindergarten students, more time to individualize educational experiences, and more time to allow children to learn through play and exploration in a rich educational environment.

Administrators and school board members with a special interest in early childhood may also recognize in full-day kindergarten a new avenue for improving educational opportunities for the children in their communities. They may see full-day kindergarten as one way to stimulate early learning and enjoyment of school in students with fewer advantages and as a way to identify earlier and to intervene more effectively with children who have exceptional educational needs. If the required space and other resources are available, local education leaders may be among the strongest supporters of full-day kindergarten.

Is full-day kindergarten the "silver bullet" of early education? Is it more powerful than other educational interventions that schools might offer for four-, five-, and six-year-olds? Probably not. I strongly encourage educators to consider full-day kindergarten as one possible element in an array of early education and family support programs that have potential to improve the long-term health and educational success of students. In addition to full-day kindergarten, other early childhood programs that are important for communities to consider include the following:

- birth-to-three-years early intervention programs for infants and toddlers with developmental delays or disabilities;
- inclusive early childhood special education programs for three- to five-year-olds;

Get the full text of "Who Will Pay for Full-Day K?" at **www.education-world.com/a_admin/admin030.shtml**

- education and support programs for new and expectant parents;
- Head Start and Early Head Start for low-income children and families;
- family literacy programs to encourage early reading;
- early intensive reading intervention programs, such as "Reading Recovery";
- preventive health care for young children; and
- communitywide efforts to improve the quality and funding base for child care for all young children.

Creating and maintaining such an array of high-quality services like these will bring about long-term positive results for the education and health of a community's children and youth. To be sure, this is no easy task! High-quality early education and care does not come cheap. It requires specially trained early education and family support professionals, a substantial funding base, and collaborative, communitywide efforts to develop an effective network of early education and family support programs. Public schools should be key collaborators in these community networks, but parents, employers, private schools, nonprofit agencies, service groups, religious groups, and health-care providers can all make key contributions. One way for public schools to provide community leadership in early education and family support is to initiate or participate in local early childhood coordinating councils. Community coordinating committees, such as the Step Ahead Councils that have been organized in every county in Indiana, typically include all of the stakeholders mentioned above.[26] Such collaborative community groups are able to work effectively to identify the needs of young children and families and to develop needed programs.

Promoting Consideration of Full-Day Kindergarten

If you are a parent, you can share this booklet with kindergarten teachers, school administrators, and school board members in your community. Urge them to consider developing an optional full-day kindergarten program. Offer to serve on an early childhood task force to research and recommend improvements in kindergarten and other early childhood programs.

If you are a teacher, use the research summarized in this booklet and other resources to initiate discussions with your teaching colleagues and your principal about full-day kindergarten and other early childhood program options (see the Internet and print resources listed at the end of this booklet).

If you are a school administrator, share this information with interested staff and parents, arrange visits to schools that already have full-day programs, and create a school or district task force to consider and make recommendations about full-day kindergarten and other early education and family support programs.

Once a community has decided to develop a full-day kindergarten option, supporters may need to work with legislators to secure state-level policy support and funding. This is especially true in states that restrict use of state funds to one-half day of kindergarten. Without full state funding, local schools may have to consider charging families tuition for a full day. This may exclude children who could benefit most from full-day kindergarten, because their families cannot afford to pay. State policy makers will need to know if full-day funding proposals have wide support among parents and teachers.

It should be clear to the reader that full-day kindergarten is not the answer to all of the problems of education. But the growth in full-day kindergarten does represent an expanding commitment to provide high-quality education and care for all young children in the United

---

Visit KidSource Online at **www.kidsource.com/ kidsource/contents3/ full.day.kinder.p.k12.3.html** to read "What Should Parents Know About Full-Day Kindergarten?"

States. Communities across America are currently taking this step, making this additional commitment. Full-day kindergarten is timely for educators, parents, and other supporters of education to consider.

ENDNOTES

1. U.S. Department of Education, National Center for Education Statistics, 1998.
2. U.S. Census Bureau, *Current Population Reports*, "Who's Minding Our Preschoolers?" 1994.
3. Rima Shore, *Rethinking the Brain: New Insights into Early Development* (New York: Families and Work Institute, 1997).
4. Robert Pianta et al., "Teachers' Judgments of Success in the Transition to Kindergarten," *Early Childhood Research Quarterly*, in press.
5. See, for example, Donna M. Bryant and Richard M. Clifford, "150 Years of Kindergarten: How Far Have We Come?" *Early Childhood Research Quarterly* 7, no. 2 (1992): 147-54.
6. Doris Pronin Fromberg, *Full-Day Kindergarten: Planning and Practicing a Dynamic Themes Curriculum*, Early Childhood Education Series, 2d ed. (New York: Teachers College Press, 1995); Dominic F. Gullo, "Changing Family Context: Implications for the Development of All-Day Kindergartens," *Young Children* 45, no. 4 (1990): 35-39.
7. Nancy Karweit, "The Kindergarten Experience," *Educational Leadership* 49, no. 6 (1992): 82-86.
8. Fromberg, *Full-Day Kindergarten.*
9. Barbara D. Day, "What's Happening in Early Childhood Programs Across the United States," in *Public School Early Childhood Programs: A Resource Guide*, edited by Cynthia C. Warger (Alexandria, Va.: Association for Supervision and Curriculum Development, 1988), 3-31.
10. Mary Renck Jalongo, "What Is Happening to Kindergarten?" *Childhood Education* 62, no. 3 (1986): 154-60.
11. Ibid.
12. Thomas A. Stinard, *Synopsis of Research on Kindergarten Scheduling: Half-Day, Every-Day; Full-Day, Alternate-Day; and Full-Day, Every-Day* (Cedar Rapids, Iowa: Grant Wood Area Education Agency, 1982). (ERIC Document Reproduction No. ED 219 151)
13. Vincent T. Puleo, "Current Research Perspectives on Full-Day Kindergarten," *ERS Spectrum* 4, no. 4 (1986): 32-38; Vincent T. Puleo, "A Review and Critique of Research on Full-Day Kindergarten," *Elementary School Journal* 88, no. 4 (1988): 427-39.
14. Nancy Karweit, *Effective Kindergarten Programs and Practices for Students At Risk* (Washington, D.C.: Office of Educational Research and Improvement, 1987). (ERIC Document Reproduction No. ED 291 835)
15. Patrick M. Bickers, *Effects of Kindergarten Scheduling: A Summary of Research. Research Brief* (Arlington, Va.: Educational Research Service, 1989). (ERIC Document Reproduction No. ED 310 852)
16. Charlene Hildebrand, "Effects of All-Day and Half-Day Kindergarten Programming on Reading, Writing, Math, and Classroom Social Behaviors," in National Forum of Applied Educational Research Journal (vol. 12E, no. 3) [electronic journal] (Lake Charles, La., 1999 [cited 18 February 2000]); available from http://www.nationalforum.com/TOCaer10e3.html.
17. Hildebrand, "Effects of All-Day and Half-Day Kindergarten Programming"; D. F. Gullo et al., "Comparative Study of 'All-Day,' 'Alternate-Day,' and 'Half-Day' Kindergarten Schedules: Effects on Achievement and Classroom Social Behaviors," *Journal of Research in Childhood Education* 1, no. 2 (1986): 87-94.
18. Joseph A. Fusaro, "Effect of Full-Day Kindergarten on Student Achievement: A Meta-Analysis," *Child Study Journal* 27, no. 4 (1997): 269-77.
19. James Elicker and Sangeeta Mathur, "What Do They Do All Day? Comprehensive Evaluation of a Full-Day Kindergarten," *Early Childhood Research Quarterly* 12, no. 4 (1997): 459-80; Hildebrand, "Effects of All-Day and Half-Day Kindergarten Programming"; Karweit, *Effective Kindergarten Programs and Practices for Students At Risk.*
20. Constance Kamii, ed., *Achievement Testing in the Early Grades: The Games Grown-Ups Play* (Washington, D.C.: National Association for the Education of Young Children, 1990).
21. Karweit, *Effective Kindergarten Programs and Practices for Students At Risk.*

22. Elicker and Mathur, "What Do They Do All Day?"
23. Sue Bredekamp and Carol Copple, *Developmentally Appropriate Practice in Early Childhood Programs*, rev. ed. (Washington, D.C.: National Association for the Education of Young Children, 1997).
24. Hildebrand, "Effects of All-Day and Half-Day Kindergarten Programming."
25. Gullo et al., "A Comparative Study."
26. Indiana Step Ahead, Office of Community Planning, Indiana Families and Social Services Administration, P.O. Box 7083, Indianapolis, IN 46207-7083. (http://www.ai.org/fssa/StepAhead/index.html)

RESOURCES

Books and Articles

Adams, Marilyn Jager, et al. *Phonemic Awareness in Young Children: A Classroom Curriculum.* Baltimore: P.H. Brookes, 1998.

Armington, David. *The Living Classroom: Writing, Reading, and Beyond.* Washington, D.C.: National Association for the Education of Young Children, 1987.

Baratta-Lorton, Mary. *Math Their Way.* Menlo Park, Calif.: Addison-Wesley, 1989. (To order catalog call 1-800-535-4391.)

Benson, Ron. *Beginnings: Teaching and Learning in the Kindergarten.* Katonah, N.Y.: Richard C. Owen, 1993.

Bredekamp, Sue, and Copple, Carol. *Developmentally Appropriate Practice in Early Childhood Programs.* Rev. ed. Washington, D.C.: National Association for the Education of Young Children, 1997.

Cherry, Clare. *Creative Art for the Developing Child.* 2d ed. Belmont, Calif.: Fearon Teacher Aids, 1990.**

Cazden, Courtney. *Whole Language Plus: Essays on Literacy in the United States and New Zealand.* New York: Teachers College Press, 1992.

Fisher, Bobbi. *Joyful Learning: A Whole Language Kindergarten.* Portsmouth, N.H.: Heinemann Educational Books, 1991.

Fromberg, Doris. *The Full-Day Kindergarten.* New York: Teachers College Press, 1987.

Goffin, Stacie G., and Stegelin, Delores A. *Changing Kindergartens: Four Success Stories.* Washington, D.C.: National Association for the Education of Young Children, 1992.*

Gullo, Dominic. "The Changing Family Context: Implications for the Development of All-Day Kindergartens." *Young Children* 45, no. 4 (1990): 35-39.

Gullo, Dominic F. *Understanding Assessment and Evaluation in Early Childhood Education.* New York: Teachers College Press, 1994.

Hamilton, Darlene Softly, Flemming, Bonnie Mack, and Hicks, JoAnne Deal. *Resources for Creative Teaching in Early Childhood Education.* 2d ed. San Diego, Calif.: Harcourt Brace Jovanovich, 1990.**

Hart, Craig H., Burts, Diane C., and Charlesworth, Rosalind. *Integrated Curriculum and Developmentally Appropriate Practice: Birth to Age Eight.* SUNY Series, Early Childhood Education: Inquiries and Insights. Albany, N.Y.: State University of New York Press, 1997.

Hendrick, Joanne. *Total Learning: Developmental Curriculum for the Young Child.* 3rd ed. Upper Saddle River, N.J.: Merrill Pub. Co., 1998.

Indiana Department of Education. *Kindergarten Guide.* Indianapolis, Ind.: Author, 1989. (Order from the Center for School Improvement and Performance, Prime Time Unit, Room 229, State House, Indianapolis, Ind. 46204-2798. Phone: 317/232-9144.)

Katz, Lilian G., and Chard, Sylvia C. *Engaging Children's Minds: The Project Approach.* Norwood, N.J.: Ablex Publishing Corp., 1989.**

Morrow, Lesley Mandel. *Literacy Development in the Early Years: Helping Children Read and Write.* 2d ed. Boston: Allyn and Bacon, 1997.

Neuman, Susan B., and Roskos, Kathleen A. *Language and Literacy in the Early Years: An Integrated Approach.* Fort Worth, Tex.: Harcourt Brace Jovanovitch, 1993.

Peck, Johanne T., McCaig, Ginny, and Sapp, Mary Ellen. *Kindergarten Policies: What Is Best for Children?* Washington, D.C.: National Association for the Education of Young Children, 1988.*

Raines, Shirley C., and Canady, Robert J. *The Whole Language Kindergarten.* New York: Teachers College Press, 1990.

Raines, Shirley C., and Canady, Robert J. *Story Stretchers for the Primary Grades: Activities to Expand Children's Favorite Books.* Mt. Rainier, Md.: Gryphon House, 1989. (Also available by same authors: *More Story Stretchers: More Activities to Expand Children's Favorite Books.* Mt. Rainier, Md.: Gryphon House, 1991.)**

Rust, Frances O'Connell. *Changing Teaching, Changing Schools: Bringing Early Childhood Practice into Public Education: Case Studies from the Kindergarten.* New York: Teachers College Press, 1993.

Schickendanz, Judith A. *Much More Than the ABC's : The Early Stages of Reading and Writing.* Washington, D.C.: National Association for the Education of Young Children, 1999.

Southern Association on Children Under Six. *The Portfolio and Its Use: Developmentally Appropriate Assessment of Young Children.* Little Rock, Ark.: Author, 1992. (Order directly from the Southern Association for Children Under Six, P.O. Box 5403, Little Rock, Ark. 72215-5403.)

Walmsley, Bonnie Brown, Camp, Anne Marie, and Walmsley, Sean A. *Teaching Kindergarten: A Developmentally Appropriate Approach.* Portsmouth, N.H.: Heinemann Educational Books, 1992.

* Available from the National Association for the Education of Young Children, the source of all NAEYC publications. To have your name added to their mailing list or request a catalog, call 800/424-2460.

** Available from Redleaf Press, source of many quality resources for early childhood professionals. To have your name added to their mailing list or request a catalog, write Redleaf Press, 450 N. Syndicate, Suite 5, St. Paul, Minn. 55104-4125, or call 800/423-8309.

Websites

http://www.naeyc.org

http://ericps.ed.uiuc.edu/eece/askeric.html

http://www.ed.gov/databases/ERIC_Digests/ed256474.html

http://www.papartnerships.org/fdkweb.htm

http://www.education-world.com/a_admin/admin030.shtml

http://www.evsc.k12.in.us/evscinfo/kindergarten/contents.html

http://www.kidsource.com/kidsource/content3/full.day.kinder.p.k12.3.html

http://www.kconnect.com/

http://www.reading.org/publications/books/lssv1_2.htm